F&SF Ministry For JESUS

NEW YORK CITY BECOMES THE CAPITAL OF THE NEW WORLD ORDER

APOSTLE FREDERICK E. FRANKLIN

authorHOUSE®

AuthorHouse™
1663 Liberty Drive
Bloomington, IN 47403
www.authorhouse.com
Phone: 1-800-839-8640

Published by AuthorHouse 10/29/2013

ISBN: 978-1-4918-2922-6 (sc)
ISBN: 978-1-4918-2921-9 (e)

Library of Congress Control Number: 2013918252

This Book Was Finalized March 1, 2000.
"New York City Becomes The Capital of The New World Order"
Was Written Between February 19 and March 1, 2000.

We encourage you to the distribution of this book through ordering
and purchasing of this book and related tapes and writings.

Profits by sales of this book or any content thereof is prohibited
except authorized by F & S F Ministry For JESUS.

CONTENTS

INTRODUCTION

This is the (33nd) thirty-second Book which we, F & S F Ministry for JESUS, have written. All of the books that we have written was a result of God giving us revelation (prophecy, words of knowledge and words of wisdom). After God would give us this revelation, He would tell us to write a book of it and reveal it to the world. This Book, "New York City Becomes The Capital Of The New World Order," has likewise, been written after revelation from God and by direction from God to write it and reveal it to the world.

In this Book we write of the prophecy that God gave us on December 2, 1999, on Thursday afternoon, between 2:00 p.m. and 3:00 p.m. It took us almost (3) three months to start writing on this book, because we did not know for sure before that time, that we were to write a Book of what God told us.

God gave us revelation on this Thursday afternoon, between 2:00 and 3:00 p.m., on December 2, 1999, concerning the New World Order. God did not use the phrase "New World Order", but, rather, He said, The Reorganizing Of The World. We have chosen, with God's consent, the wording "New World

Order" because it is a phrase the world is familiar with. God told us on this Thursday afternoon, at least (7) seven major prophecies related to how the New World Order would be.

In this Book we provide you with the prophecies that God gave us on December 2, 1999, with revelation that He has given us in the past. This provides a clear picture of the establishment of the New World Order and the dismantling of the New World Order. This is a very important Book. We are sure that your eyes will be opened to the future like never before. We show New York City's role in New World Order. We show the United States' role in the New World Order. We provide you with the name of the most important people in the New World Order. Much, very much more, we provide.

NEW YORK CITY BECOMES THE CAPITAL OF THE NEW WORLD ORDER

We write this Book due to revelation given to us directly from God on December 2, 1999, at about 2:00 p.m. to 3:00 p.m. This day, Thursday, December 2, 1999 will be forever in our remembrances, for this is the day that someone who was/is very dear to our hearts died. She died at the age of (101) one hundred and one years old.

On this sunshiny late fall afternoon at about 2:00 p.m. of December 2, 1999, God began to speak to us. God told us how the New World Order would be organized. God let us know that New York City and not Washington, D.C., as presently is the case, will be the most powerful location on earth. The United States is the super power of the world and its Capital, Washington, D.C., is the headquarters of power. For many years there have been certain ones who jokingly suggested that the capital of the United States should be moved to New York City. Although they suggested it, we do not believe that they actually thought that such a move could or would actually take place. They concluded that since New York City was the greatest city on earth, then it should be Capital. After all, they concluded, why should not New York City have the seat of power in the world, in that, Wall Street and the stock market is in New York City; it is the center of commerce; it is headquarters for the major media outlets; it represents the door of immigration into the United States; and, even, the United Nations headquarters is located in New York City. Although it has been thought to be the logical place for the seat of power of the world to be located, in New York City, it is doubtful, however, that anyone actually thought it would replace Washington, D.C., but it will happen.

God also told us on this December 2, 1999, Thursday afternoon between 2:00 p.m. and 3:00 p.m., that the countries of the world would become as states of the United States, with their capital being New York City. God further let us know at this time that the United Nations, which is located in New York City, will be the governing body of the different transformed country states. The United Nations governing the different transformed country states would be in similar manner as the Congress of the United States governs. God provided further prophecy to us and told us that the different leaders of the countries would merely be as governors.

These governors would be similar as the governors of different states of the United States.

God also prophesied to us telling us on this Thursday afternoon between 2:00 and 3:00 p.m. on December 2, 1999, that Bill Clinton, President Bill Clinton would be the President of the world. God told us Bill Clinton would be the President in the New World Order over the transformed country states. He will be President over all the different leaders of the countries which will become states. President Bill Clinton will be over the United Nations.

God told us President Bill Clinton's headquarters will be in New York City. President Bill Clinton's political career is not coming to an end as has been said, but rather his greatest political career is yet to come. As he has been the greatest President that the United States has ever had, he will become the greatest political leader and President that the world has ever known. He will surpass the political leaderships of the Pharaohs Egypt, Alexander The Great and the Creasers of Rome. God further told us on this December 2, 1999, Thursday, afternoon, between 2:00 p.m. and 3:00 p.m. visitation, confirming what he had told us before, that, Bill Clinton as President of the whole world, would be second in power only to Pope John Paul II. God told us that Pope John Paul II will be worshipped as God by the whole world. All that the evil that Bill Clinton will do will be directed by Pope John Paul II. All that Pope John Paul II does will be directed by Satan. For those of you who have read and received the writings of our previous books, what we have now written in this Book should fill in the blanks concerning your end time understanding. We, however, understand that what we have said thus far that God told us might not be believed by many. So, let us go back and analyze each prophecy that we say that God told us. Let us see is it contrary to the word of God. Let us even see if it seems logical.

To analyze what we have said that God told us of the future on December 2, 1999, between 2:00 p.m. and 3:00 p.m., on that Thursday, let us first discuss what we have said about Pope John Paul II and President Bill Clinton. By understanding Pope John Paul II's and President Bill Clinton's Biblical identification, then the prophecies given to us can at least be understood and hopefully believed.

We are prophets of God and God has revealed much of the future to us concerning Biblical end time events. God has given us this revelation and told us to write this Book and reveal it to the world. The revelation has been extensive. This is now our (33nd) thirty third Book that we have written. All of about two or three of our books are writings concerning end time events. In the back of this Book is a listing of our books, which we have written. In our previous books we wrote that God told us Carof Josef Woityla, Pope John Paul II, is the man that will be the so-called Anti-Christ. God has now told or shown us more than (20) twenty times that Pope John Paul II, Carof Josef Woityla, is so-called Anti-Christ; it is he that is the man mentioned in the Holy Bible as the Abomination of Desolation, Vile Person, King, Son of Perdition, Little Horn and Beast. He will be the evil ruler over the entire world during a (3 ½) three and one-half year period called the Great Tribulation. He will deceive the world that he is God. He will persecute and have killed many that will not worship him as God. Those that worship him will have a (666) six hundred and sixty-six mark put on their foreheads or in their hands.

Revelation Ch. 20, V. 2
"… the dragon, that old serpent, which is the Devil, and Satan…"

Revelation Ch. 13, Vs. 4 & 5
"And they worshipped the dragon which gave power unto the beast: and they worshipped the beast saying "Who is like unto the beast? Who is able to make war with him? And there was given

unto him a mouth speaking great things and blasphemies; and power was given unto him to continue <u>forty and two months</u>."

<u>Revelation Ch. 13, V. 8</u>
"And all that dwell upon the earth shall worship him, whose names are not written in the book of life..."

<u>Revelation Ch. 13, V. 2</u>
"...and the dragon gave him his power and his seat, and great authority."

<u>Revelation Ch. 13, V. 14</u>
"And deceiveth them that dwell on the earth..."

<u>Revelation Ch. 20, Vs. 4 & 5</u>
"...and I saw the souls of them that were beheaded for the witness of Jesus, and the word of God, and which had not worshipped the beast, neither his image, neither had received his mark upon their foreheads, or in their hands; and they lived and reigned with Christ a thousand years. But, the rest of the dead lived not again until the thousand years were finished. This the first resurrection."

<u>Revelation Ch. 13, V. 16</u>
"... causeth all, both small and great, rich and poor, free and bond, to receive a mark in their foreheads..."

Refer to our books:

1. "Proof That Your Leaders Have Deceived You And The End Times."

2. "What God Is Now Telling His Prophets About The End Times."

3. "The Name of The (Anti-Christ) Beast and 666 Identification."

We show you in the Book, The Name of The (Anti-Christ Beast) And 666 Identification", How Pope John Paul II is a perfect match to the scriptures throughout the Bible related to identifying the (Anti- Christ) Beast. We also show how Pope John Paul II's name equal to (666) six hundred and sixty-six.

Revelation Ch. 13, V 18
"Here is wisdom. Let him that hath understanding count the number of the beast: for it is the number of a man; and his number is six hundred threescore and six."

For those of you who do not know, to take the 666 mark, will seal your fate in hell. You will burn in fire forever and ever.

Revelation Ch. 14, Vs. 9,10 &11

"... If any man worship the beast and his image, and receive his mark in his forehead, or in his hand,... he shall be tormented with fire and brimstones... And the smoke of their torment ascendeth up forever and ever: and they have no rest day or night, who worship the beast and his image, and whosoever recieveth the mark in his name."

We have written much concerning President Bill Clinton in our previous books which God told us concerning him. God told us early in the year 1992 that Bill Clinton would narrowly defeat President George Bush and Ross Perot and be elected as President of the United States. We wrote about this and preached about it before it happened. God also told us that Bill Clinton would beat Bob Dole and be re-elected as President of the United States. God told us early in the year of the election. We also wrote about all of this and preached about this before it happened.

President Bill Clinton has accomplished more than any other President of the United States have accomplished. When Bill Clinton, Governor Bill Clinton, was running for his first term as President of the United States, his critics and Republican opponents said that if he would become President then the stock market would fail and there would be a great depression. Well, before Bill Clinton was elected as President, during George H. Bush's Presidency, the country and world was continually in and out of recessions or depressions. The Stock Market's highest levels had been around 3,000. This is the highest it had reached since its continual existence starting in 1896. Since President Bill Clinton's term in office, there has been no depression. There has not yet even been one recession. Not only that, the Stock Market has reached a height of over 11,000. For the first time since 1969 the United States' budget was balanced. The unemployment level has been 4%, the lowest in 30 years. Before Bill Clinton took office, Black unemployment was over 14%. As of January, 2000, Black unemployment was 8%, the lowest on record. As of January, 2000, Hispanic unemployment was just over 6%, less than 6.5%. This was the lowest on record.

During President Bill Clinton's tenure in office, the inflation level has been at the lowest levels it has been in over 30 years. Before and even after, he was elected as President, his critics said there would be a war against the United States by Russia because of Bill Clinton's lack of military experience. Well, there has been no war with Russia and the United States has been at peace for the entire two terms of Bill Clinton's Presidency. Since his Presidency, Russia has continued to decrease and the United States has continued to increase. We could go on and on talking about President Bill Clinton and how he has proved his critics wrong.

President Bill Clinton through his leadership role with the government and private industry and the business world, has solved what was alleged to be the most destructive potential problem of modern times. It was said, mainly by his Republican opponents, that President Bill Clinton would not be able to solve this problem and it would result in worldwide destruction. We are talking, of course, about the Y2K problem. Well, the Y2K problem was resolved without the least problem occurring. It was resolved in the United States and all over the world. Even in China there was no problem. It was predicted that there would especially be terrible problems in the very large and less prepared China. A certain Electrical Engineer with a major business of the United States performed an exceptionally outstanding job in resolving the Y2K problem in China. By the way, that Electrical Engineer was a college classmate of mine, my buddy Foy. It turned out that the China's Y2K problem was resolved before many of the others and work on this project served as a model to resolve the Y2K problems elsewhere. Without President Bill Clinton's policy of engagement with China, the Y2K problem would not have been solved. This in itself, could have led to a worldwide disaster.

We wrote in our First Book " Proof That Your Leaders Have Deceived You And The End Times." that one of the first actions that President Bill Clinton performed, after his inauguration, was to commission Vice President Al Gore to computerize the United States. Refer to our books:

1. "Proof That Your Leaders Have Deceived You And The End Times."

2. United States In The Bible."

The effort that President Bill Clinton initiated to computerize the United States resulted in the fast development of the internet which caused a worldwide revolution. He has caused financial prosperity during his term as President through his decisions and policies like the world has never known. He has solved conflicts throughout the earth that were said to be impossible to resolve. During the end of President George H. Bush's Presidency, he said that there was no solution to resolving the conflict in Bosnia. Shortly into his, Bill Clinton's, first term as President, the conflict was resolved. All the world renowned military leaders and authorities/strategists said that President Bill Clinton was absolutely wrong in thinking that he could win a war with air bombing only. Well, he proved them wrong and rewrote the book in military strategy. In a few weeks he won the war against Serbia and Milosevic and without a solider on his side being killed in combat. This was a first and one of a kind historical triumph. His critics said that even though he won the war, that they said could not be done, he could not get the people back to their homes before the harsh winter would kill them. President Bill Clinton got them all back to their homes before the harsh winter conditions started.

Who then is Bill Clinton? Who then is the former Rhodes Scholar? Who then is Bill Clinton, whose childhood and family background should have made it impossible for him to become the President of the United States? Who then is Bill Clinton who is politically successful against all odds? Who then is this Bill Clinton, of whom the Republican Party of the United States is jealous? Who then is this Bill Clinton, that even mighty media (television, radio, newspapers, etc.) of the United States with all of its continued efforts, could not get out the office through impeachment? Who then is this Bill Clinton that is successful where all others have failed? Who then is this Bill Clinton that the media (television, radio, newspaper, etc.) predicts time and time again will lose, but yet he wins? Who then is this Bill Clinton, that seem not to be affected no matter how long and intense is the pressure? Who then is this Bill Clinton, that dared to challenge the powerful strongholds of the tobacco companies and (NRA) National Rifle Association and was not destroyed? Who then is this Bill Clinton, that destroyed the invisibility of NRA Nation Rifle Association? Who then is this bill Clinton that God told us about on December 2, 1999, between 2:00 and 3:00 p.m. on that Thursday, would be the President of the whole world?

God told us back in the <u>first part of the year 1995</u> that President Bill Clinton will be the second beast of Revelation, Chapter 13, which is the false Prophet of Revelation, Chapter 19. He will be the one that administer all the evil on behalf of the (Anti-Christ) Beast, Pope John Paul II, Carol Josef Wojtyla, during the Great Tribulation. Refer to our Book "Who Is The (False Prophet) Second Beast?"

<u>Revelation Ch. 13, V 11</u>
"And I beheld another beast coming up out of the earth; and he had two horns like a lamb, and he spake as a dragon."

Revelation Ch. 13, V. 12
"And he exerciseth all the power of the first beast before him, and casueth the earth and them which dwell therein to worship the first beast, whose deadly wound was healed."

The word "exerciseth" in the above Scripture means to administer. Bill Clinton will administer the evil on behalf of Pope John Paul II, Carol Josef Wojtyla.

Revelation Ch. 13, Vs. 15,16 & 17
"And he had power to give life unto the image of the beast, that the image of the beast should both speak, and cause that as many as would not worship the image of the beast should be killed. And he causeth all, both small and great, rich and poor, free and bond, to receive a mark in their right hand, or in their foreheads: And that no man might buy or sell, save he that had the mark, or the name of the beast, or the number of his name."

Revelation Ch. 13, Vs. 13 & 14
"And he doeth great wonders, so that he maketh fire come down from heaven on the earth in the sight of men. And deceiveth them that dwell on the earth by the means of those miracles which he had power to do in the sight of the beast; saying to them that dwell on the earth, that they should

make an image of the beast, which had the wound by the sword and did live."

<u>Revelation Ch. 19, V. 20</u>
"And the beast was taken, and with him the false prophet that wrought miracles before him, with which he deceived them that had received the mark of the beast, and them that worshipped his image..."

You might say and others have said, that you cannot see how Bill Clinton could be known as a prophet, false or otherwise. We say to you, we showed in our Book, "Who Is The (False Prophet) The Other Beast", how the prophet title is associated with Bill Clinton. We will not rewrite this Book, we suggest that you read it. Also read our Book "What God Is Now Telling His Prophets About The End Times". We have spared no effort to make this very important Book available in print electronically through the Internet and in print, including in paperback. Also with the case with this Book, we have had certain publications get put in large print. This will help those that have difficulty in reading small print. We also put this Book on audio tape and CD for those who do not desire or cannot read.

We said that God told us that Bill Clinton would narrowly defeat President George H. Bush and Ross

Perot, and it came to pass. We said that God told us that President Bill Clinton would defeat Bob Dole and be re-elected as President, and it happened as we said. God showed us that President Bill Clinton would be limping due to his leg being hurt, we said what God told us and it happened. God showed us that senator McClanahan of New York, Senator Kerrey of Nebraska and Senator Lieberman of Connecticut would have a news conference on television denouncing President Bill Clinton's actions concerning a sex scandal and it came to pass just as we wrote and preached that God showed us. God showed me this in a trans. God showed us this back in the summer of 1997. Much more has God shown or told us about President Bill Clinton, some of it we have written in our Books:

1. Proof That Your Leaders Have Deceived You And The End Times."

2. The United States In The Bible."

3. What God Is Now Telling His Prophets About The End Times."

4. Who Is The (False Prophet) Second Beast"

5. "Why When and How The (Anti-Christ) Beast Will Deceive The World He Is God"

6. The Ten Horns Of The Book of Daniel And Revelation"

7. "The Judgment Of The United States"

8. Other(s)

If you understand who President Bill Clinton is, then you can understand all that he has done and accomplished. President Bill Clinton has had destiny on his side. You can then understand how Bill Clinton's childhood and family background did not prevent him from becoming President of the United States. You can then understand how President Bill Clinton has been politically successful against all odds. You can then understand how he can be so amazingly successful that it makes his opponents of the Republican Party jealous and envious of him; you can understand why he yet prospers politically while his very powerful opponents of the Republican Party have failed by the way; such as George H. Bush, Bob Dole, Newt Gingrich, Kenneth Star, Bob Livingston, Henry Hide, etc. Knowing that President Bill Clinton is the (False Prophet) Second Beast, you can then understand how the mighty media (television, radio, newspapers, etc.) of the United States, with all of it continued efforts could not get him out of office through impeachment. You can then understand how he has been successful where all other have failed. You can then understand how he continually wins when the mighty media (television, radio, newspaper, etc.) predict time and time again that he will lose. You can then understand how he seems not to be affected no matter how long and intense is the pressure. You can then understand how he dared to challenge the powerful strongholds of the Tobacco Companies and (NRA) National Rifle Association. President Bill Clinton is a man of destiny.

We wrote in Chapter 6 of our first Book " Proof That Your Leader Have Deceived And The End Times" that Satan could not find a better candidate than Bill Clinton to do his will. The powers that be, that make up this evil and powerful place called the United States, is a mixture of evil and cunning people. Bill Clinton is the one person that is most capable of this mixture. Although his opponents do not want to admit it, Bill Clinton is what is known in this world as a genius. However, the wisdom of this world is foolishness to God. God, also, said that the just/righteous is wise; Bill Clinton is certainly not just/righteous. He, however, seems always to be at least (10) then steps ahead of all his political opponents. This is because he is more cunning than they are or they are that stupid. President Bill Clinton has been chosen by God to fulfill certain of his words. Even as Pharaoh of Egypt was chosen by God to fulfill his word so that Moses could deliver Israel out of bondage, likewise, has President Bill Clinton been chosen. Although President Bill Clinton is the servant of Satan, God, however chose him. Jesus said that he chose (12) twelve disciples and one of them was a devil. He was speaking of Judas Iscariot the betrayer.

John Ch. 6, Vs. 70 & 71
"Jesus answered them, Have not I chosen you twelve, and one of you is a devil? He spoke of Judas Iscariot the son of Simon: for he it was that should betray him, being one of the twelve."

Revelation Ch. 17, V. 17
"For God has put in their hearts to fulfill his will, and to agree, and give their kingdom to the beast, until the words of God shall be fulfilled."

Psalm Ch. 75, Vs. 6 & 7
"For promotion cometh neither from the east, nor from the west, nor from the south. But God judge: he putteth down one, and setteth up another."

Those of you who have been President Bill Clinton's Republican political opponents might be tempted to boast because of your efforts against him, we say that, you probably could not be in his position because you are a hypocrite and not smart enough.

Except you repent, be born again, and obey God, the lake of fire will be your fate and ultimate destiny also.

God has not shown us yet, how this will soon come about, but soon President Bill Clinton's Republican opponents along with most of the rest of the world will love him. Yes! We said love him!

If we said God told us the things we mentioned earlier, and they came to pass, you should be convinced that Bill Clinton will be the (False Prophet) Second Beast. We have a proven track record of us saying God said, and it came to pass. One of the notable events that we prophesied was that O.J. Simpson would have a verdict of innocent in his widely media covered criminal trial. We, likewise, wrote about it before it happened and it came to pass.

Now that you understand that Pope John Paul II, Carol Josef Wojtyla, is the (Anti-Christ) Beast and President Bill Clinton is the (False Prophet) Second Beast, you can then see the likehood of the rest of the prophecies given to us by God on December 2, 1999 on Thursday between 2:00 and 3:00 p.m. are true. One other thing that would be helpful to your understanding, if you realized the Biblical importance and identity of the United States. The

Biblical identity of the United States was revealed unto us by God in year of 1992. We have written about the identity in our books:

1. Proof That Your Leaders Have Deceived You And The End Times."

2. The United States In The Bible."

3. What God Is Now Telling His Prophets About The End Times."

4. "The Judgment Of The United States"

5. "The Horns Of The Books Of Daniel And Revelation"

6. Others.

God showed us a dream back in the Year of 1992 that the United States was the Great Babylon of the Book of Revelation of the New Testament of the Holy Bible. In the dream, God showed us a very large Book with very many pages in it. This Book contained every event of mankind's existence. God opened up the Book to the back part of it. As he would turn the pages of the Book, what was written in printed words would come alive. It was if the printed words would turn into a very large movie screen. God showed us many things that would happen in the future as he would turn the pages of the Book. We will not tell you at this time all God showed us. We, however, will mention a few words of revelation concerning our visitation with God. As God turned the pages of this very large Book and the words of print continued to appear as a very large movie screen, God showed us fire and explosions somewhere on earth. God showed us missiles flying through the sky and this was what was causing the fire and explosions. They were aligned in formation continually coming from somewhere. The flying missiles look to be similar to birds flying in formation during winter migration. The missiles were of the nuclear and poison gas variety. The bombardment was continual and devastating. Then God showed us the place of this bombardment was the United States.

After this we saw, in the very large movie like vision, large fowl such as cranes, geese, etc. They were nasty looking and sickly looking. They were vomiting and just filthy. They were deformed and look to be retarded. God showed us that the fowl were all nasty, sickly, vomiting, filthy, deformed and retarded looking because of contamination due to the nuclear poison gas bombardment. God showed where this event was located in the Bible. God led us to Revelation Chapter 18, Verse 2.

Revelation Chapter 18, V. 1 & 2

"And after these things I saw another angel come down from heaven, having great power; and the earth was lightened with his glory. And he cried mightily with a strong voice, saying, Babylon the great is fallen, is fallen, and has become habitation of devils, and the hold of every foul spirit, <u>and a cage of every unclean and hateful bird.</u>"

The birds mentioned in above scripture are unclean and hateful due to nuclear contamination that God showed us in the vision of the dream.

Revelation Chapter 18, V. 8

"Therefore shall her plagues come in one day, death and mourning, and famine; and she shall be utterly burned with fire: for strong is the Lord God that judgeth her."

Revelation Chapter 18, Vs.17 & 18

"For in hour so great riches is come to naught. And every shipmaster, and all company in ship, and sailors, and as many as trade by sea, <u>stood far off.</u> And cried when they saw the smoke of her burning, saying, What city is like unto this great city!"

When the above scripture said "stood afar off," this was the indication of the fear of the people of getting contaminated by nuclear and poison gas contamination.

The United States in the Bible is called by the names of Great Babylon, Babylon, Great City, Whore and Woman. See Revelation, Chapters 16, 17, 18 and 19.

Now that you understand that Pope John Paul II, Carol Josef Wojtyla, is the (Anti-Christ) Beast, President Bill Clinton is the (False Prophet) Second Beast and the United States is the Great Babylon, the rest of what God told us in prophecy on December 2, 1999, between 2:00 p.m. and 3:00 p.m., should be at least understandable. We said that God told us during this time that New York City would replace Washington D.C. as the center of power on earth. We can see activity towards this end already starting. Recently, under the initation of President Bill Clinton, for the first time in its existence, a United States Senator addressed the United Nations on policy direction in its building in New York City. By now, President Bill Clinton might understand who he is. He might realize that he is to be the leader of the world for the (Anti-Christ) Beast, Pope John Paul II, Carol Josef Wojtyla. If this is so, this would be another of President Bill Clinton's foresighted efforts. There might be other visits by Congress members, of others of power and influence of the United States, to address the United Nations. As the nature of a politician is, one would much rather make a speech to a world audience versus a mere national audience. This in itself provides a measure of power for the United Nations of New York City over the power of Capital Hill of Washington, D.C. Another effort that point to New York City becoming the seat of world political power through the United Nations, can be seen through President Bill Clinton and Hillary Rodham Clinton buying a house in New York. Mrs. Clinton's effort in announcing her running for Senator in New York is an effort that further points to the rising of political power in New York City.

We, also, told you that God told us on December 2, 1999, on Thursday, 2:00 and 3:00 p.m., that President Bill Clinton would be as President over the entire world through the United Nations. By now, since you now understand that President Bill Clinton will be the (False Prophet) Second Beast, this should only seem appropriate. God has not, yet, shown us the details of how this will happen, but we know it will happen. President Bill Clinton's efforts in initiating the communication and economic revolution through the Internet will make him an attractive candidate for this position of world dominance. Also, his efforts in tearing down worldwide trade barriers will aid in his acceptance. Further, his worldwide leadership of military victory of matchless and strategy transforming exploits against Serbia and Milosevic will aid in his acceptance. We do not know how it will happen, but God told us back in the Year of 1996, that President Bill Clinton would turn over the military of the United States to the United Nations.

We also said that God told us December 2, 1999, on Thursday, between 2:00 and 3:00 p.m., that the different countries of the world would be as states under the United Nations. They will be states similar to the United States individual states. Also, we said that God told us that the different leaders (President, Kings, etc.) over the transformed country states will be merely as governors similar to the governor of the states in the United States. Their leader/president will be President Bill Clinton. Their god will be Pope John Paul II, Carol Josef Wojtyla. The above status of states, governors, leader/president and god, is the New World Order. New York City will be the Capital of the New World Order.

We can see certain activity that has already begun that will lead to transforming the countries to a state-like status. Any diminishing of sovereignty helps bring about this transformation. When President George H. Bush brought all the world together to go against Iraq and Saddam Hussein in the Gulf War, this was the beginning of the establishment of the New World Order. Each country involved gave up a certain sovereignty to the United Nations. President Bill Clinton's efforts in eliminating trade barriers between the different countries will help lead to this state-like status. Like always, here is President Bill Clinton carrying out plans for the big picture. Unlike what President Bill Clinton's political opponents thought they understood, his ultimate goal has not been to make himself a great President of the United States, but rather to position himself to be the President of the world. He has positioned himself to be the President/Leader of the New World Order.

The Holy Bible shows evidence of the sovereignty of the countries being diminishing in the last days. Both the Books of Daniel and Revelation indicate this diminished status. In the Book of Daniel, the Prophet Daniel had a dream from God showing that the (Anti-Christ) Beast, which is the Little Horn, which is Pope John Paul II, Carol Josef Wojtyla, take over the control of three major countries. He will establish a worldwide empire with these three countries and seven other countries. He allow for a certain time, until the very end, these other seven countries to be governed by their existing leaders. One of the three countries will be the

United States. We believe the other two countries of the three could be Great Britain and Russia. This is what the theologians say about the lion and bear. Without contrary revelation from God, we agree that it could be so. We, however disagree with who they say that the little horn is. Contrary to what they say, the leopard is the United States. Refer to our Book "The Ten Horns Of The Books Of Daniel And Revelation."

Daniel Ch. 7, V. 3
"And four beasts came up from the sea, diverse one from another."

The word "sea" in the above scripture represents the multitude/masses of people on earth.

Daniel Ch. 7, V. 17
"These great beasts, which are four, are four Kings which shall arise out the earth."

Daniel Ch. 7, Vs. 4-6
"The first was like a lion… a second like to a bear… and lo another, like a leopard…"

Daniel Ch. 7, Vs. 7 & 8
"After this I saw in the night visions, and behold a fourth beast… strong exceedingly… and it had ten horns. I considered the horns and behold, there came up among them another little horn…"

Daniel Ch. 7, V. 24

"And the ten horns out of this kingdom are ten kings that shall arise: and another shall rise after them, and he shall be diverse from the first, and he shall subdue three kings."

Daniel Ch. 7, V. 12

"As concerning the rest of the beasts, they had their dominion taken away: yet their lives were prolonged for a season and time."

The rest of the beasts mentioned in the above Scripture are the first three beasts. These are the lion, bear and leopard. God has revealed to us that the leopard is the United States. Scriptural evidence that it is the United States can be seen in Daniel Chapter 7, Verse 6, when it says that this leopard had dominion. This dominion represents the United States as the Super Power of the world.

Daniel Ch. 7, V. 6

"... and dominion was given to it."

For more details proving that the leopard is the United States, refer to our Books:

1. "The Ten Horns Of The Books Of Daniel and Revelation"

2. "The Judgment Of The United States"

We said we believe that the other beasts of the three, could be Great Britain and Russia. The lion could be Great Britain because it has been called lion. The bear could be Russia because it had been called a red bear.

Earlier in a Scripture, it indicates that the President/ Leader/King of the Kingdoms of the first three beasts would be removed from their positions by the (Little Horn) Pope John Paul II, Carol Josef Wojtyla.

Daniel Ch. 7, V. 12
"As concerning the rest of the beasts, they had their dominion taken away: yet their lives were prolonged for a season and time."

The above Scripture indicates that a future President of the United States would be removed from his Office by Pope John Paul II, Carol Josef Wojtyla, depending on when the Great Tribulation starts. We emphasize "depending on when the Great Tribulation starts". God has not yet shown us a date when the Great Tribulation will start. However, God showed us in our Book "Proof That Your Leader Have Deceived You In The End Times," Chapter 7, that the Great Tribulation cannot start to The Temple in Jerusalem is rebuilt. Refer to it. God has not shown us, yet, who the President who will be removed will be, but we know that he will. Its kind of ironic, out of all efforts that was made to remove Bill Clinton from Office that was not successful, he along with Pope John Paul II, Carol Josef Wojtyla, will remove a future President from Office. Depending on when the Great Tribulation starts. Not only will they remove that President from office, they will kill that President. That President along with the leaders at that time of Great Britain and Russia, will be killed after (15) fifteen months of their removal. Time as used in in the Scriptures is a year and a season is 3 months. There are 12 months in a year. There are four different (3) three month seasons in a year. For proof/verification concerning this representation, refer to Daniel Ch. 7, V. 25; Daniel Ch. 12, V. 7; Revelation Ch. 12, Vs. 6 and 14. The Book of Revelation of the New Testament of the Holy Bible, further shows the United States is the leopard of Daniel Chapter 7. We have shown that the United States is the Great Babylon. The Great Babylon is the one that has dominance in the last days. Remember, Great Babylon is also called the woman.

Revelation Ch.18,Vs. 3,7, 10 &11
"...and the merchants of the earth are waxed rich through the adundance of her delicacies. How much she hath glorified herself and lived deliciously...

that great city Babylon, that mighty city! For in one hour is thy judgment come. And the merchants of the earth shall weep and mourn over her; for no man buyeth their merchandise anymore..."

<u>Revelation Ch. 17, V. 18</u>
"And the woman which thou sawest is that great city, which regineth over the Kings of the earth."

The above scriptures in Revelation Chapter 17 and 18, further indicates the diminishing of sovereignty of the countries, referring to even the most powerful of the once country as a city.

Some of you might wonder, why is it that the (Great Babylon) United States will get destroyed? In our Book, "The judgment Of The United States," we tell you why it will be destroyed. We provide several reasons why God has been, is, and will be displeased with the United States, which will result in its destruction. The Pope and Bill Clinton will have it destroyed for a totally different reason why God Almighty will be using them to destroy it. We suggest that everyone read this Book. This Book is essential reading for those that live in the United States. It is ordained by God for the United States to be destroyed. The United States was allowed to be established to fulfill the word of God. The main reason why the United States will be destroyed is because it will be the slaughtering place of God's saints during the Great Tribulation.

Revelation Ch. 18, V. 20
"Rejoice over her, thou heaven, and ye holy apostles and prophets; for God hath avenged you on her."

Revelation Ch. 18, V. 24
"And in her was found the blood of prophets, and of saints, and of all that were slain upon the earth.

Revelation Ch. 20, V. 4
"...and I saw the souls of them that were beheaded for the witness of Jesus, and for the word of God, and which had not worshiped the beast, neither his image, neither had received his mark upon their foreheads, or in their hands..."

Daniel Ch. 11, Vs. 32 & 33
"...but the people that do know their God shall be strong, and do exploits. And they that understand shall instruct many: yet they shall fall by the sword, and by flame, by captivity, and by spoil, many days."

As the above scripture in Daniel Chapter 11 indicates, the saints of God will teach the truth on letting the world know the truth on salvation. That is, you must speak in tongues and be baptized in the name of Jesus to be saved. Also, we of God's saints will continually be telling the world that the

Great Tribulation is before First resurrection, the so-called rapture. We, also, as God's saints, will continually be letting the world know that Pope John Paul II, Carol Josef Wojtyla, is the (Anti-Christ) Beast and that Bill Clinton is the (False Prophet) Second Beast.

It is because of this continual preaching of the truth by the saints of God that will cause the United States to be destroyed. Although the United States would have served Pope John Paul II, Carol Josef Wojtyla, very well, to shut up the mouth of the saints of God, he will sacrifice it by having it destroyed. Again, God uses those of the world to carry out his will.

It makes no difference to Pope John Paul II, Carol Josef Wojtyla, that he will be killing millions of his followers that worship him as God in the United States, he will yet have it destroyed. To destroy a relatively few saints of God, he will destroy that many of his own followers who have taken his 666 mark. This is typical action of Satan to destroy his followers after he has deceived and used them. Since Pope John Paul II, Carol Josef Wojtyla, will be Satan's body on earth, then it only follows that he the (Anti-Christ) Beast should do likewise. God in his great wisdom uses the people's false god to punish them. The United States has been and will be the most evil place the world has ever known. It will receive its just reward. The United States is worse than Sodom and Gomorrah. It is worse than the society/world of Noah's day. They were destroyed by God due to their widespread evil. The United States commits widespread evil of all they did and the people pretend to be righteous. The United States is a land of religious hypocrisy.

<u>Revelation Ch. 17, Vs. 16 & 17</u>
"And the ten horns which thou sawest upon the beasts, these shall hate the <u>whore,</u> and shall make her desolate and naked, and shall eat her flesh, and burn her with fire. For God hath put in their hearts to fulfill his will, and to agree, and give their Kingdom unto the beast, until the words of God shall be fulfilled."

The ten horns in the above Scripture are not the same as the ten horns that was mentioned earlier in the Book of Daniel. These ten horns of the Book of Daniel will be replaced by the ten horns of the Book of Revelation. The ten horns of Daniel were reigning Kings. The Pope John Paul II, Carol Josef Wojtyla, by this time would have long since removed three of the ten horns which we mentioned earlier. Pope John Paul II, Carol Josef Wojtyla, will install the new ten horns at the very end for the specific purpose of destroying the United States.

Revelation Ch. 17, V. 12

"And the ten horns which thou sawest are ten Kings, which have received no kingdom as yet; but received power as Kings one hour with the beast."

To see why Pope John Paul II, Carol Josef Wojtyla, removed the ten horns in the Book of Daniel, refer to our Book "The Ten Horns Of The Books Of Daniel And Revelation."

Although the Pope, Pope John Paul II, Carol Josef Wojtyla, and Bill Clinton, will have the United States destroyed in an effort to destroy the saints of God, we believe that by the time that the bombs hit the United States that the saints of God would have been taken up from the earth in the so-called rapture, the First Resurrection.

I Thessalonians Ch. 4, Vs.16 & 17

"For the Lord himself shall descend from heaven with a shout, with the voice of the archangel, with the trump of God: and the dead and Christ shall rise first: Then we which are alive and remain shall be caught up together with them in the clouds, to meet the Lord in the air: and so shall we ever be with the Lord."

Remember what we said when God opened up the very larger Book to us and we saw explosions on the United States? Well, the view that was shown to us of this particular event was from far above in the sky. This could have been our view in the First Resurrection, so-called rapture, when we meet the Lord in the air. Another reason we believe and in fact, we know that the bombing of the United States to destroy the saints will be after the First Resurrection, so-called rapture, is because this destruction is part of the period of the Wrath of God. God through Apostle Paul wrote that the saints of God would be protected from/escape the wrath of God.

I Thessalonians Ch. 5, V. 9
"For God has not appoint us wrath, but to obtain salvation by our Lord Jesus Christ…"

Revelation Ch. 16, Vs. 1 & 19
"And I heard a great voice out of the temple saying to the seven angels, Go your ways, and pour out the vials of the wrath of God upon the earth. And the great city was divided into three parts, and the cities of the nations fell: and Great Babylon came in the remembrance of God, to give unto her the cup of wine of the fierceness of his wrath."

The Great Tribulation is before The First Resurrection, so-called rapture, and is before the Wrath of God.

There is one place in Scriptures of the Holy Bible that indisputably shows that the Great Tribulation is before the First Resurrection, so-called rapture. God revealed this to us back in the middle to late 1980's. By the time God showed us this, there had been many debates by theologians and others of whether or not the Great Tribulation was before the so-called rapture, the First Resurrection. What God revealed to us had never been used to show that the Great Tribulation will, indeed, be first and therefore those that said the so-called rapture, the First Resurrection, was first always won the debates. The indisputable scriptures that show that the Great Tribulation is before so-called rapture, the First Resurrection, God showed us was located in the Book of Revelation Chapter 20, Verses 4,5, and 6. In these Scriptures, it shows that those who would not worship the (Anti-Christ) Beast, Pope John Paul II, Carol Josef Wojtyla, during the Great Tribulation would have their heads cut off and they would be in the so-called rapture, the First Resurrection; which are the dead in Christ rising first. In order for them to get their heads cut off in the Great Tribulation and yet be in the so-called rapture, the First Resurrection, means that the Great Tribulation would have to be before the First Resurrection, so-called rapture.

Revelation Ch. 20, Vs. 4,5 & 6

"...and I saw the souls of them that were beheaded for the witness of Jesus, and for the word of God, and which not worshiped the beast, neither his image, neither had received his mark upon their hands; and they lived and reigned with Christ a thousand years. But, the rest of the dead lived not again until the thousand years were finished. This is the first resurrection. Blessed and holy is he that hath part in the first resurrection: on such the second death hath no power, but they shall be priests of Christ, and shall reign with him a thousand years."

I Thessalonians Ch. 4, Vs.16 & 17

"For the Lord himself shall descend from heaven with a shout, with the voice of the archangel, and with the trump of God: and the dead in Christ shall rise first: Then we which are alive and remain shall be caught up together with them in the clouds, to meet the Lord in the air: and so shall we ever be with the Lord."

If there are yet those of you who incorrectly believe that the so-called rapture, the First Resurrection, is before the Great Tribulation, we suggest that you read our Book, "Main Arguments For The Rapture Being Before The Great Tribulation, And Why They Are Not True." When the (Anti-Christ) Beast,

Pope John Paul II, Carol Josef Wojtyla, and (False Prophet) Second beast, Bill Clinton, eventually destroy the United States, this will be the initial efforts in destroying the New World Order. This will end New York City's role as being the capital of the New World Order. It is even fitting symbolically that New York City be the center of power that is located in the United States and it is located in the New York City area. The great statue opens the door to New York City. The Statue of Liberty symbolically represents the United States and is located in the New York City area. The great Statue, idol god, opens the door to New York City and the United States. Remember, the Biblical name of the United States is Great Babylon. Great Babylon is also called the woman. The Statue of Liberty is a statue of a woman.

Revelation Ch. 17, V. 18
"And the woman which thou sawest is that great city, which reigneth over the Kings of the earth."

Revelation Ch. 17, Vs. 5 & 6
"And upon her forehead was a name written, MYSTERY, BABYLON THE GREAT, THE MOTHER OF HARLOTS AND ABOMINATIONS OF THE EARTH. And I saw the woman drunketh with the blood of the saints, and with the blood of the martyrs of Jesus..."

In our Book, "The Judgment Of The United States" we show how the symbolic names in the above Scriptures are associated with the United States.

For those of you who are not familiar with the writings of the Holy Bible, you might be wondering what will be the fate of the (Anti-Christ) Beast, Pope John Paul II, Carol Josef Wojtyla, and the (False Prophet) Second Beast, Bill Clinton. Well, these two devils will not escape punishment.

Revelation Ch. 19, V. 19
"And I saw the beast, and the Kings of the earth, and their armies, gathered together to make war against him that sat on the horse and against his army."

Jesus/God is the one "that sat on the horse." His army are the angels and saints of God that were taken up in the, so-called rapture, the First Resurrection. Read verses 11 through 16 of Revelation Chapter 19.

Revelation Ch. 19, V. 20
"And the beast was taken and with him the false prophet that wrought miracles before him, with which he deceived them that had received the mark of the beast, and them that worshipped his image. These both were cast alive into a lake of fire burning with brimstone."

Revelation Ch. 20, V. 10

"And the devil that deceived them was cast into the lake of fire and brimstone, where the beast and false prophet are, and shall be tormented day and night for ever and ever."

The New World Order's destruction will be completed with this battle in which the (Anti-Christ) Beast, Pope John Paul II, Carol Josef Wojtyla and the (False Prophet) second Beast, Bill Clinton, are taken and cast into the lake of fire and brimstone. Unlike what has been taught by the false prophecy teachers, the Battle of Armageddon will not end (7) years after the so-called rapture, First Resurrection. This time cannot be more than slightly less than (45) forty-five days. We prove that it will only be a few weeks.

Refer to our Books:

1. "Proof That Your Leaders Have Deceived You and The End Times."

2. What God Is Now Telling His Prophets About The End Times"

3. "How Long Will It Be Until The End"

4. "When The End Will Come"

The New World Order is finished with the ending of the Battle of Armageddon.

APOSTLE FREDERICK E. FRANKLIN'S TESTIMONY

Let me give you my personal testimony. Let me tell you about how I got filled with the Holy Ghost. Back in 1985 I lived in Washington, D.C. I was not married at that time. It was in October of 1985. I had my own business as a Utilities Engineering Consultant. As a sinner and as usually was the case, I left out of a certain bar around 1:00 am. When finally I reached the place where I was living and was opening my door, the telephone began to ring. I went in and answered the telephone. It was my first cousin calling from Mobile, Alabama. He, also, was about high and was just getting in from a bar. As usually was the case, we started talking about God. We knew little to nothing about God, but somehow we always started talking about God. As we talked, I started talking about the preachers of God. I said that those O lying preachers that say they lay hands on people and they get healed are the worst ones. I said only Jesus could heal someone like that. I at least knew that Jesus could heal like that. My cousin said you are right. Two drunks talking. He then said the only other ones who could do that were Peter, John, Paul and the other Apostles of the Holy Bible. I was shocked. I was so shocked that I got sober. I said what! What! He said yes! Peter, John, Paul and the other Apostles laid hands on the people and they got healed. I was totally astounded! I was totally amazed! I was sober!

After we hanged up the telephone, I went and picked up the Bible which I had kept with me since about 1963. I had never opened the Bible I was just religious and kept it with me. I had been putting off reading it for all these years. When the urge would come to me to read it, I would put it off to the next month, or next week, or next day, or when I finished a certain project, or when I finished during this or that. I did not know it then, but I know now, the urge was God trying to get me to read the Bible. I finally dusted off and opened that Bible. It was now around 2:00 am. I wanted to see for myself where it said that a man could lay hands on a person and he or she could get healed. I was after all, an Electrical Engineer and this was illogical. How could flesh, blood and bones heal someone? It did not make any sense. Not having any idea where to look, I searched and searched and searched. I read and read and read. Finally, somewhere between 3:00-4:00 am, I found it. I saw that Peter laid hands on people and they got healed. It was amazing! It was like a very bright light was turned on in my head. I was speechless. To understand the greatness of my astonishment, you need to understand my childhood hopelessness. I, as a child, being black brought up in Alabama, living far out in a rural area, started working when I was four years old. I would go outside of our house at night, walking through the woods, looking up in the sky at the moon and the stars, and ask God why? I knew it had to be a God. I would ask God why would he leave his children down on this earth at the mercy of Satan? Satan of course, I knew, had no mercy. I could not understand why. Everything that seemed to be good, appeared to be on Satan's side. The evil people had it. White folks had it who were doing evil. Why, why, why, was my question? I never received an answer. It appeared that God could care less about the suffering of and in justice to his children on this earth.

When I saw that someone could get healed by another just by laying hands on them, then I understood clearly the answer to my why. I understood that God had not left us at the mercy of Satan. I, however, wanted to see could anyone lay hands on people and they could get healed. As I continued to search and read, now about day break, I "discovered" that you had to have the Holy Ghost to be able to heal. I wanted then to see could anyone receive the Holy Ghost. Now far in the morning of the next day, I "discovered" that anyone could receive the Holy Ghost. I "discovered" that you spoke in tongues when you received the Holy Ghost. My life desire would never be the same again. I wanted to see how I could receive the Holy Ghost. I learned that you had to repent. So, I asked God to forgive my sins. Then I asked God to give me the Holy Ghost, let me speak in tongues. Nothing happened. I did not speak in tongues. All that day I was asking God to forgive my sins and to let me speak in tongues. I did not work that day. This went on all day and into the night. Nothing ever happened. Exhausted I fell asleep into the next morning. When I woke the next day I started doing the same thing. I asked God to forgive my sins and let me speak in tongues. Nothing happened. I thought that maybe I need to read God's word and then I might receive the Holy Ghost. So, I read several Books of the Bible. Then I asked God to forgive my sins and let me speak in tongues. Nothing happened. I did this over and over each day and nothing ever happened. I had stop working all together. To receive the Holy Ghost was the most important thing in my life. I made a pledge to God that I would not go to the bars again. Nothing happened as I sought for the Holy Ghost. I made a pledge to God to stop drinking and stop smoking marijuana. Nothing happened. I made a pledge to God to stop fornicating. Nothing happened as I sought for the Holy Ghost. I was praying for the Holy Ghost and reading God's word and nothing happened. I decided to read the whole Bible. I read from Genesis through the Book of Revelation and nothing happened as I sought for the Holy Ghost during that time. Now it was the end of the year of 1985 and nothing happened as I sought for the Holy Ghost. I decided to move from Washington, D.C., back to my house in Montgomery, Alabama. Now after reading the whole Bible, I was praying about (22) twenty two hours a day to receive the Holy Ghost and nothing happened. I started crying and praying and nothing happened. I had only cried (4) four times in my life. I remember all the way back from (2) two years old. Crying and seeking for the Holy Ghost is all I did. I never spoke in tongues. This crying and seeking God for the Holy Ghost reached now into August of the year 1986. I had counted all of the months, weeks, and days to that time of seeking for the Holy Ghost, now seeking about (22) twenty two hours a day. I had about (3) three months before, cleaned out my house of everything that I thought was sinful. I threw away all pornography, whiskey, wine and beer, marijuana and whatever I thought was sinful into my trash can. I did this and nothing ever happened. Now here it was in August, seeking to speak in tongues and I had not. I said, I thought, that maybe I need to join a Church. This might would help, I thought. I looked into the yellow pages of the phone book and chose (4) four churches that I would check out to join. This was now August 3, 1986. I was still seeking God for the Holy Ghost. I still was crying and praying to speak in tongues about (22) twenty two hours a day. On August 3, 1986, I turned on my television early in the morning and turning the channels I saw and heard some ridiculous sounding Church Choir singing with the TV camera shaking. I stopped to see what in the world would this be on television so unprofessional. I was amazed. I had once worked at a television station in Cleveland, Ohio, and I was just amazed at this. As I looked and listened in amazement, a young woman came before the camera to introduce/present her Apostle. She said that her Apostle laid hands on people, preformed many miracles and prayed for many to receive the Holy Ghost. This really caught my attention. I thought, could this be the answer to my quest? Then her Apostle came forth. A black, tall, old man, Apostle William A. Tumlin. I had already decided that I wanted to join a church under an old man who really knew something about God. Also, I wanted it to be a small church. I did not want anything to be like that Baptist Church that I was brought up in. All they cared about was looks, a big choir, a big church, a big funeral, always looks. They cared about looks, but yet certain ones was committing adultery and it seemed to be alright. Many were drunks and it seemed not to matter. I was brought up in this and had not learned hardly anything that I had finally read in the Bible.

Yet seeking God for the Holy Ghost, on August 10, 1986, I decided to first check out this Church and Apostle that I had seen on Television, before checking out the other churches. I went to the Church and it was a small church. I went into the Church and the Apostle preached and asked did anyone want to join the Church, I to my amazement went up and join the Church. I thought that the Apostle would pray for me to receive the Holy Ghost, but he did not. I was confused. After the service was dismissed, I went to the Apostle's wife and told her that I wanted to receive the Holy Ghost. She said, Oh, I thought you already had the Holy Ghost. She told me to go and tell the Apostle. I went to the Apostle and said I want to receive the Holy Ghost. He said Oh, I thought you already had the Holy Ghost. He said come back, either next Sunday or that afternoon before the 6:00 taping of the radio broadcast, and he would pray for me to receive the Holy Ghost. I said that I would come back before the taping of the broadcast. I was not about to wait for a whole week. I could tell you how many months, weeks and days I had been seeking for the Holy Ghost. I had been seeking for the Holy Ghost every day since October of 1985 and it was now August 10, 1986.

When I went home from Apostle Tumlin's Church, The All Nations Church of God, I did something that was key to me receiving the Holy Ghost. Remember I told you that I threw away all, pornography, whiskey, wine, beer, marijuana and other things I thought was sinful into my trash can. Well, I went back to my trash can and I got (2) two marijuana joints out of it and brought them back into my house. I had stop smoking marijuana during my time of seeking the Holy Ghost and had no intentions of smoking anymore. I did not know it at that time, but I know it now, it was Satan that convinced me to get those (2) two joints out of my trash can. I thought, Satan told me, that I might need them if I got a headache. I just had them in my closet in case I might need them for a headache. The Devil, Satan, just made a fool out of me. The only time I had those headaches is when I had a hangover. I was not going to have a hangover because I had stop drinking. What a fool. However, on August, 10, 1986, before I went back to receive the Holy

Ghost, it had to be God who told me, I went to my closet and got those two joints and flushed them down my toilet stool. When I did this, it felt like a very, very, heavy weight was taken off me. At 5:00 on August 10, 1986, I was back at Apostle Tumlin's Church, The All Nations Church of God, to receive the Holy Ghost. I went in the Church and sat down in about the fourth row of the pews, next to the aisle, on the left side looking from the pulpit. There were about (3) three to (4) four people in the sanctuary, including the Apostle's wife. They were there praying. However, the Apostle was nowhere to be seen. I sat there waiting for the Apostle and he never showed up. It was now 5:30 pm and there was no sign of the Apostle. I was getting very anxious because the radio broadcast's taping was to start at 6:00 pm. Finally, the Apostle came out of a room from the front of the Church. I was so excited! I finally was going to receive the Holy Ghost! The Apostle walked towards me and down the aisle and right by me and went into the rest room near the entrance to the Church. He did not say one word to me. Not even a gesture toward me. Some minutes past by and he was still back there. I just kept praying. I just kept repenting. Finally he came out. He came to the back of me and put his hands on my head and said receive the Holy Ghost. I was excited and nervous. I did not know what to expect. Then with his hands on my head, he said speak in tongues. I said to myself, what is this man talking about? I said to myself, you have to receive the Holy Ghost before you speak in tongues. He, the Apostle, just kept saying speak in tongues. Then he, with hands on my head, started speaking in tongues. Then he said receive the Holy Ghost, speak in tongues. Then he started speaking in tongues. Then he said speak in tongues with his hands on my head. Then to my amazement he began to give up on me and remove his hands, I stood up so his hands could not be removed. I thought to myself, no, no, you are not going to give up on me this quick. So he let his hands stay on my head and began to speak in tongues. Then he said speak in tongues. I by this time, with the Apostle's hands on my head, was standing in front of the church facing the pews, but I did not know it. He said again speak in tongues. I said to myself this is not working, I am going to get out of here. I said to myself, the next time that he speaks in tongues I am just going to mimic him and pretend that I have the Holy Ghost so I can leave. He then spoke in tongues. Then I went to mimic him. The next thing I knew, I was speaking in a language that sounded like Hebrew, before the audience of people in the Church, motioning my hands like I was before them teaching them something. Then

I said to myself, what in the world am I doing. This was totally unlike me. Then the Apostle said, you have been filled with the Holy Ghost. Then all of a sudden I stop speaking this Hebrew like language. The Apostle just kept saying you have been filled with the Holy Ghost. I was saying to myself, is this what it is to be filled with the Holy Ghost? I did not know what to say. I did not know what to think. I went and sat back down in the same place that I was sitting before. By this time, it was time for the taping of the radio broadcast. As I sat there, Satan began to talk to me. He told me that I did not have the Holy Ghost. He said that as evil as I had been, that God would not give me the Holy Ghost. Satan then brought up to me every evil thing that I had done. He kept saying, you do not have the Holy Ghost. This went on for about an hour as I sat there. After the taping was over and I left the Church, Satan kept up his accusations and saying that I did not have the Holy Ghost. All the way as I drove home, he kept it up. When I entered into my house I said to God that if I received the Holy Ghost, let me know without a shadow of doubt. Immediately I began to speak in tongues. I was speaking loud in tongues. I began to analyze this speaking. I was not trying to mimic. My mouth and tongue were moving and I was not trying to make them move. I was speaking sounding eloquently, whatever I was speaking. This speaking went on for about an hour with me analyzing to see whether it was me or God speaking. I then thought that I might not be able to stop speaking in tongues. Immediately I stop speaking in tongues and God spoke to me clearly and said that my name had been written in the Book of Life and everything has been worth it. I knew what God meant by worth it and I started crying. All of these months. All of these weeks. All of these days. All of the praying. All of the crying. All of this seeking for the Holy Ghost, but it is worth it. Later on I would get baptized by the Apostle in the name of Jesus Christ for the remission of my sins.

This one thing I want to point out. I could have received the Holy Ghost, all the way back in October of 1985, if I had got rid of that dope and the other things of sin. You cannot hold on to the past, anything of the past that is sin, and receive the Holy Ghost. Satan would have caused me to go to hell over (2) two marijuana joints. Two joints would have kept me from immortality.

PROPHETESS SYLVIA FRANKLIN'S TESTIMONIES OF RECEIVING THE HOLY GHOST

When my wife, Prophetess Sylvia Franklin, was a child she had a very depressing life. There was constant arguing and fighting between her father and mother. Her father would be drunk and pull out a gun and threaten to kill her mother and even at certain times to kill her and her brother.

At (10) ten years old, Sylvia would look out of her window and look up and ask God to take away the gloom and let the sun shine. She always would do this. It always seemed to be so gloomy in those days. As time went by in this constant state of family turmoil, at (13) thirteen years old, God did let the sun shine in Sylvia's life. After Sylvia, her mother and brother started attending a small Holiness Church, Sylvia was involved with a street meeting service. This was Apostle William Tumlin's Church. During the meeting the people were singing and praising the Lord. Sylvia then started singing and praising the Lord and all of a sudden she started speaking in tongues.

Not really understanding what had happened to her, Sylvia was in and out of Church. As time passed Sylvia lost the Holy Ghost. At (17) seventeen years old Sylvia was in a service at Apostle William A. Tumlin's Church, All Nations Church of God. While singing and praising was taking place in the Church, Apostle Tumlin came to where Sylvia was and laid hands on her head and she started speaking in tongues. She was restored in the Holy Ghost. Later on she got baptized by Apostle Tumlin in the name of Jesus Christ for the remission of sins. Sylvia's life was never the same again.

Our Oldest Child ELIJAH JEREMIAH EZEKIEL FRANKLIN'S Testimony of Receiving the Holy Ghost

On January 31, 1995 our son, Elijah Jeremiah Ezekiel Franklin, had his fifth birthday. This is the same child the doctors said would have only a ten percent or less chance of being born. This is the same child some would have recommended being aborted (murdered in the womb). This is the same child who is in very good health. This is the same child the doctors said would have probable extreme health problems. This is the same child who was born premature.

After turning five years old, two days later on February 2, 1995, while we (Frederick and Sylvia) were praying for him in our house during our weekly Thursday night prayer service, he was filled with the Holy Ghost. He spoke in tongues for about an hour. After he finished speaking in tongues, we baptized him in the name of Jesus.

Through the testimony of Elijah's salvation, other children have desired to be saved and were indeed filled with the Holy Ghost and baptized in the name of Jesus.

NOTE THIS. Two Days After Elijah Spoke In Tongues, He Prophesied And Said, God Is Saying To Him, That We Would Be Moving To A Farm In Mobile, With Farm Animals. Later On That Year, In October, We Moved To That Farm.

DANIEL ISAIAH FRANKLIN'S and REBEKAH ANNA FRANKLIN'S Testimonies of Receiving the Holy Ghost

This dedication is to give praise and glory to God Almighty, Father Jesus our Lord and Savior and to his Son Jesus Christ of whom the Father dwelled in on this earth, for the born again experience of Daniel Isaiah and Rebekah Anna.

June 15, 1998 was a special day in our family. This is the day that we completed household salvation in our family, the day that we could say that all five of us were born again. On this day, June 15, 1998, as we all prayed fervently during our daily dedicated afternoon prayer, God moved mightily in our presence. We were already excited for the young woman that we had prayed to receive the Holy Ghost the past night which we were preparing to baptize after our prayer time.

As we prayed fervently for God to move in a special way that day for the souls to be saved in our community, God spoke to us to pray for Daniel and Rebekah. We, Frederick, Sylvia and Elijah, started praying for them to be filled with the Holy Ghost. As we prayed, we noticed that Daniel and Rebekah were under the influence of the presence of God in praising him and they began to speak in tongues. We wondered could this actually be happening this fast as we had been praying for? Could our five year old son and four year old daughter now finally be filled with the Holy Ghost? We had been praying to God every day since they were conceived in Sylvia's womb for them to receive the Holy Ghost. We didn't really know whether they were speaking in tongues or not at this time because during prayer our children often would mimic us when we were speaking in tongues. But, this time seemed to be different, especially with Rebekah. Daniel Isaiah, every since he was about one year old, always has fervently praised the Lord, singing, dancing, lifting up his hands to God and appearing to speak in tongues. Rebekah, however, did not normally praise God as enthusiastically as did Daniel. But on this day, June 15, 1998, at about 2:00 p.m., our little Rebekah was on fire! And even the normally enthusiastic Daniel seemed to have a double portion. We looked at them and wondered could this actually be it? Could our Daniel Isaiah be filled with the Holy Ghost? Could our son, who was born three months premature, be now born again of the Spirit? Could our son, who at one time only weighed (2) two pounds and (13) thirteen ounces, be born again of the Spirit? Could our son, who the doctors said would have to stay in the hospital for at least three months after he was born, who only stayed one month because he was so healthy, could he actually be speaking in tongues? Could this, our son who is strong and in excellent health who doctors said would have severe and numerous health problems, be born again of the Spirit? Could it also be that our little Rebekah be born again of the Spirit? Could it be that the Daddy's little girl, that he calls "Pretty Pretty" be born again of the Spirit? Could both Daniel Isaiah and Rebekah be filled with the Holy Ghost? Could Frederick now release our second book for publication after waiting for Daniel and Rebekah to be born again so he could dedicate some pages in the book to their born again experience as he had done in our first with Elijah?

We did not want to make a mistake here and tell Daniel and Rebekah that they had been filled with the Holy Ghost, it was too important. We had to be sure. So, we prayed to God for him to tell us clearly whether they had been filled with the Holy Ghost or not.

God answered us quickly and said yes. We were exceedingly glad and satisfied. But, to our shame and astonishment, God also said that Daniel had been filled with the Holy Ghost before now. God did not tell us when, neither did we know. We suspected it was during one of our weekly Thursday night prayer services or during one of our three daily prayer times. God would later let us know that Daniel had received the Holy Ghost when he was (3) three years old during one of our weekly night services. Although we were shamed and rightly so, for not knowing our son was already filled with the Holy Ghost, our joy was rekindled and we went immediately and baptized Daniel Isaiah and Rebekah Anna in the name of Jesus for the remission of their sins to complete their born again experience.

REASONS TO WANT TO BE SAVED

Why would you want to be saved? Well, I will give you three good reasons to want to be saved. You might say, I don't need to be saved. You might say, I'm doing just fine like I am. Well, you might have an argument if you could guarantee the future would be what you want it to be. You might have an argument if you could guarantee that you will be living next year. You might have an argument if you could guarantee that you will be living next month. You might have an argument if you could guarantee that you will be living next week. You might have an argument if you could guarantee that you will be living tomorrow. You might have an argument if you could guarantee you will not die today. You might have an argument if you could guarantee that you will not die the next hour. You might have an argument if you can ensure that you will be living the next five minutes. If you had control over your time of life, you might not need Jesus' salvation. But, since Jesus, the God Almighty, has control over your appointed time of life, if you are not totally stupid, then you should realize that you need to be saved.

This is the bottom line, either ignorance or stupidity causes you not to get saved. Jesus, the God Almighty, before the world was created, assigned an appointed time for each of us to be born. He, also, set the exact time of our death. Jesus has assigned us our parking meter of life. Who is familiar with a prepaid cell phone? Well, for a prepaid cell phone, you have an allotted amount of minutes to use your cell phone. Once you have used all of your minutes, it is useless. It is dead. Well, Jesus, the God Almighty, has assigned us our prepaid cell phone of life. Do you know how many minutes you have left? Supposed you have (15) fifteen minutes left. Suppose (10) ten. Suppose (5) five. Do you know whether an earthquake will now occur at this place or not? Do you know whether an airplane will now or not crash into this building? Do you know whether a terrorist will now or not blow up this building? Jesus knows. Do you know whether you will or will not fall dead in this minute of a heart attack? Do you know on the way from here whether you will have an head on collision with another vehicle and be killed? Jesus knows. Your time clock of life is running out!

The number one trick of Satan is to convince those that are not saved, who want to be saved, that you have more time, until your parking meter of life expires. He hopes to convince you that you have more time, until your prepaid cell phone of life is used up.

You might be one of the fools that might say, that you do not care whether you die without being saved. If this is you, you are indeed a fool. One of the main reasons to get saved is to stay out of hell. If you are one of the ones that say you do not care whether you die without being saved, then you probably do not understand that there is a hell with a wide opened mouth waiting to swallow you. Hell is a real place. When death occurs, you, the real you, your soul, will either go to hell or heaven. If you are saved, you go to heaven. If you are not saved, you go to hell. What is hell, you might ask? Hell is a place where souls are tormented with fire. A very, very, very, hot fire. The hottest fire that we can make on earth, spirits can touch it, walk in, lay on, etc., without it burning them. Spirits are beings that include angels and devils. God, also, is a spirit. Hell is so hot that it burns spirits. Not God, but other Spirits. A person's soul is spirit. A person's soul is the person's desire, feeling, emotions, mind, hearing, sight, taste, smell and memory. The real person. The real you. The body dies and rots. The soul is eternal. It will live either in hell or with God, forever and ever more. Hell is a place located in the center of the earth. Those that are in hell are in continual torment. They are burning continually. There is no relief. Just continual screaming and burning. No rest day nor night. There is no water. There is no air conditioner. There is no fan. There is no kind of cooling. Remember, understand, that they have their feelings in hell. Remember, understand, that they have their desires in hell. Their desire to quench their thirst can never be satisfied. Their desire to alter their circumstances can never be done. Their desire to leave hell will never be fulfilled. They will be in their forever. Their cry out to God for help will be in vain. Hopelessness! Hopelessness! Hopelessness! Pain of burning continually. The pain from a burning fire, if not the worst, is one of the worse pains that you can have. Pains on your hands. Pains on your feet. Pains on your arms. Pains on your legs. Pains on your back. Pains on your belly. Pains on your chest. Pains on your face. Pains on your ears. Pains on your tongue. Pains on the top of your head. Pain everywhere. Pains all the time. All day and all night forever and ever and ever and ever and evermore. They had an alternative, they had another choice, they could have gotten saved.

This is the second good reason to want to get saved. For those of you that believe that there is a God, then you should want to be saved for your love to God. You know that God is a good God, the good God. You know that God has been good to you. You cannot live without God. You cannot walk without God. You cannot talk without God. You cannot eat without God. You cannot sleep without God. You cannot love without God. You cannot be loved without God. You cannot breathe without God. All of these things and many, many, other good things God provides you. And, not only you, but all others even his enemies. Even those that curse him. Even those who prefer to serve Satan rather than God himself. It was God who protected you from death. It was Satan who tried to kill you. It was God who healed you. It was Satan that made you sick. It was Satan who killed your love ones. It was God who protected your love ones from Satan that allowed them to live as long as they did.

To get saved is to show your love and gratitude to God. To get saved is to show your love and gratitude to God for a price that he paid for your salvation. The price was very great. God allowed his Son Jesus of Nazareth to die. There have been some men who have allowed their sons to die for what they considered a good cause or for a friend. God allowed his son to die for his enemies. God, even, allowed his Son to suffer for his enemies. To suffer such suffering never suffered before. Unbearable sufferings. God allowed him to be slapped. God allowed him to be spit on. God allowed his beard to be pulled off of his face, causing pain and bleeding and swelling. God allowed a crown made of thorns to be put on his head. Shoved into his scalp and forehead, causing pain, bleeding and swelling. God allowed his Son to be beat with (39) thirty-nine strokes of a whip that would snatch the meat off his bones. Pain, excruciating pain, bleeding and swelling. God allowed him to be nailed on a tree in his hands and feet, causing pain, excruciating pain, bleeding and swelling. God saw his son suffer. He saw his body bleed, from the top of his head to the bottom of his feet. God saw his Son's body swell, from the top of his head to the bottom of his feet. God saw his Son's body from the top of his head to the bottom of his feet change to a painful black and blue-like color with pain and red with blood. He saw him agonize in pain and misery, until through the bleeding and swelling he was not recognizable as a man. We would not and could not allow our sons and daughters, who we loved, to suffer even for a friend, let along their enemies. All that God has done for us, so much, and He only requires for a token of love, for us to accept his glorious salvation. For us to stay out of hell. So, for those who believe that there is a

God, God Almighty, then our love for God should make us want to be saved. To get saved is to show that God's sacrifice of His Son was not in vain with us. This salvation of ours makes God's investment yield a return. So great investment for such a little return. Without your salvation the little return is even smaller. Just think, by getting saved, the God that created the universe will allow us to be with him for ever and ever more. It will not be just any existence, but God has promised us in the Holy Bible, that we will have no more sorrow, no more pain, no more crying and no more death. I believe that God has allowed me to experience how it will be in heaven. Not long after I was filled with the Holy Ghost, while living in Montgomery, Alabama, God gave me a visitation. While sitting in my bed, with my legs and my feet in the bed, eyes wide opened, the presence, the glory, the anointing of God, moved on me. I felt it. I knew somehow it was God. I don't know how I knew, but I knew without a shadow of doubt that it was God. The sensation, the feeling, started at the bottom of my feet. It then covered my feet. It proceeded up my legs. It continued up my body. It covered my thighs. It just continued to go up my body. It covered my belly and chest. Then it went in my shoulders and through my arms, hands and fingers. It went up my neck and covered my head. It was all over me.

Let me try to tell you how it felt. Words cannot properly explain how good it felt. This felt at least a hundred times better than the best feeling I have ever had. There is nothing we have experience to compare with it. Let me tell you this. Everything on me felt good. My fingernails, even, felt good. My hair, even, felt good. Even each strand of hair felt good. It felt so good until I started asking God to allow those that I knew to experience it. I started calling out their names for God to allow them to feel it. I mentioned my mother, brother, sisters, grandmother, nieces, nephews, aunts, uncles, first cousins, second cousins, other relatives, friends, co-workers, college classmates that were friends, church members and maybe some others, for God to allow to experience what I was feeling. I don't know the exact time, this feeling, this presence, this anointing, this visitation, lasted. It was a long time. Maybe an hour or longer. I believe God allowed me to experience what heaven feels like. People, if this is what heaven feels like, this along is worth getting saved for.

Now I will address the third good reason to get saved. If you are one who thinks that to be saved has no present life benefit, consider this. Soon in these days, there will be a great tormenting plague to cover the whole earth. This will happen very soon. Possibly, during George W. Bush's time as President. This torment will be excruciating pain. This pain will be continual. It will affect all ages, babies, young children, teenagers, young adults, middle age adults, senior citizens, all. The pain of this plague will be so horrible, until the people will want to die. People will want to commit suicide. There will be no medicine for cure. There will be no medicine for relief. There will be screaming all over the earth. The children will be screaming. The parents will be screaming. The grandparents will be screaming. The great grandparents will be screaming. The nurses will be screaming. The doctors will be screaming. Those of the police force will be screaming. Those of the army will be screaming. Those of the Air Force will be screaming. Those of the Navy will be screaming. Those of the Marines will be screaming. The members of the House of Representatives will be screaming. The Senators will be screaming. The Supreme Court Justices will be screaming. The Vice President will be screaming. The President will be screaming. The Pope will scream. All will scream!

All of this paining. All of this misery. All of this hurting and no relief. No relief for five months. Yes! It will last for (5) five months. And think about this. It is hard to get sleep when you are in pain.

What hopelessness. The curse of this plague will be so bad that people will want to die. However, the curse of this plague will not allow them to die. This curse has been told about in the Book of Revelation of the Holy Bible. Turn to the Book of Revelation in your Bible. Look at Chapter (9) Nine. Read Verse (6) Six.

Revelation Ch.9, V.6
"And in those days shall men seek death, and shall not find it; and shall desire to die and death shall flee from them."

This great excruciating painful plague will soon happen. This painful plague will be the closest thing to hell itself. It will be so horrible, so excruciating, that God told me to write a book about it to warn the people. This is the book here. The name is "Five Month Desire To Die, But Not Possible When Fifth Angel Blows Trumpet." The only ones on planet Earth that will not be affected with this great painful plague, will be those that have the Holy Ghost. You must have the Holy Ghost to be saved. All that have the Holy Ghost speak in tongues.

If you, yet, after reading this, due to some custom, tradition or religion, do not get saved, it is because you are too stupid to get saved.

THE FOUR EASY STEPS TO GET SAVED/BORN AGAIN:

1. Repent:

    a. ask God to forgive your sins, ask in the name of Jesus;

    b. surrender your will for God's will to be done in your life.

2. Ask God to save you, to fill you with the Holy Ghost, ask in the name of Jesus.

3. Do not ask God anymore to save you, just thank God, praise God for saving you. You must thank God in the name of Jesus. At the point of your greatest sincerity, you will speak in another language. This will be your sign of confirmation. God will be using your mouth to speak a language spoken somewhere on earth that you have not learned. This is your sign that you are born of the Spirit.

4. Get baptized in the name of Jesus Christ.

John Ch.3,Vs.3&5

"Jesus answered…Except a man be born again, he cannot see the kingdom of God…Jesus answered… Except a man be born of water and of the Spirit he cannot enter into the kingdom of God."

John Ch.3,V.8

"...thou hearest the sound thereof...so is everyone that is born of the Spirit."

Colossians Ch.3,V.17

"And whatsoever ye do in word or deed, do all in the name of the Lord Jesus..."

LIST OF BOOKS THAT
WE HAVE WRITTEN

1. Proof That **YOUR LEADERS** Have **DECEIVED YOU** And The End Times

2. What **GOD** Is Now Telling His Prophets **ABOUT** The **END TIMES**

3. Five Month **DESIRE TO DIE**, But Not Possible When Fifth Angel Blows Trumpet

4. **GOD's** Word Concern **MARRIAGE AND DIVORCE**

5. The Name Of The (Anti-Christ) Beast And **666** Identification

6. **WHERE GOD's PEOPLE** (Saints) **GO** When GOD Comes Back To Get Us

7. How You Can **PROVE** That **YOU HAVE** A **SOUL**

8. **JESUS** Was **NOT CRUCIFIED WHEN** As Has Been **TAUGHT**

9. Reasons For **JEWS** To Believe That **JESUS** Is The **MESSIAH**

10. **THE** Big **LIE**

34. **MARCH** Was When **JESUS** Was **BORN** And **NOT CHRISTMAS**

35. **GOD'S FOUR** Healings And Deliverances Which He **DESIRES FOR US**

36. The Parallel/Comparison Of **JEWS AND BLACK PEOPLE** Of The United States

37. The **CHRONOLOGICAL ACCOUNT** Of The Gospels Of What Is Said **ABOUT JESUS**

38. **TIMES** That **GOD APPEARED UNTO US**

39. The **WHOLE WORLD** Becoming **AS SODOM**

40. The **TWO** Main **REASONS CMMUNION** Is To Be **TAKEN**

41. The **DOOR IS CLOSING ON** The Last Opportunity For **IMMORTALITY**

42. (**CONFIDENTIAL—(ONLY FOR THE 15 APOSTLE)** — "**APOSTLES HANDBOOK** Of Ministry Tasks Before & During The Great Tribulation")

43. **WORDS FROM GOD** By God Appearing To Us Or Just Talking To Us, **FOR THE END TIMES**

44. **GOD SAID BLACK PEOPLE** In The United States **ARE JEWS**.

HOW TO GET SAVED

To Be Saved You must Speak with Tongues & Be Baptized in the Name of Jesus

John Ch. 3, V. 3
"Jesus answered... Except a man be born again, he cannot see the Kingdom of God."

John Ch. 3, V. 5
"Jesus answered... Except a man be born of water and of the Spirit, he cannot enter into the Kingdom of God."

Acts Ch. 2, V. 38
"... Repent, and be baptized every one of you in the name of Jesus Christ for the remission of sins, and ye shall receive the gift of the Holy Ghost."

How to Repent: (1) Sincerely ask God to forgive your sins, ask in the name of Jesus; (2) Surrender your will for God's Will to be done in your life.

After Repenting: Sincerely ask God to save you, to give you his Spirit, to give you the Holy Ghost, to have you to speak with other tongues. [Once you have asked, then just continue to thank God for doing so, just praise him, sincerely. You WILL then speak in tongues.]

John Ch. 3, V. 8
"... thou hearest the sound thereof...so is everyone that is born of the Spirit."

After Speaking in Tongues: Get baptized in the name of Jesus, again you must be repented.

NOTE: You can be baptized and then receive the Holy Ghost or be filled with the Holy Ghost then be baptized.

Speaking in Tongues: Speaking in tongues (unknown language) is God speaking through you.

Mark Ch. 16, V. 17
"And these signs shall follow them that believe... they shall speak with new tongues."

Acts Ch. 2, V. 4
"... and began to speak with other tongues as the Spirit gave them utterance."

Acts Ch. 22, V 16
"... be baptized, and wash away thy sins..."

Colossians Ch. 3, V. 17
"And whatsoever ye do in word or deed, do all in the name of the Lord Jesus..."

The name of the Father is Jesus, the name of the Son is Jesus, the name of the Holy Ghost is Jesus.

John Ch. 17, V. 26
"And I have declared thy name unto them…"

John Ch. 5, V. 43 "
"I am come in my Father's name…"

Hebrews Ch. 1, V. 4
"… he hath by inheritance obtained a more excellent name…"

John Ch. 4, V. 24
"God is a Spirit…"

Question: Is the Father Holy? Answer: Yes. God is a Father; God was manifested in flesh as a Son; God is a Spirit, the Holy Spirit, the Holy Ghost.

I, Frederick E. Franklin, am a Father, am a Son, am a Human Being. Father, Son, Holy Ghost and Father, Son, Human Being are titles. God's name is Jesus.

Matthew Ch. 28, V. 19
"… Teach all nations, baptizing them in the name of … the Son…"

To Be a Part of the F&SF Ministry for JESUS the Following Will Be Expected

<u>II Timothy Ch.2, V.3</u>
"Thou therefore endure hardness, as a good soldier of Jesus Christ."

<u>Ephesians Ch.6, V.10</u>
"... be strong in the Lord, and in the power of his might."

<u>Ephesians Ch.5, V.27</u>
"That he might present it to himself a glorious church, not having spot, or wrinkle, or any such thing; but that it should be holy and without blemish."

The F&SF Ministry For JESUS Soldier Will:

1. Be Filled With The Holy Ghost (Evidenced By Speaking In Tongues)

2. Be Baptized In The Name Of JESUS

3. Be Honest And Sincere

4. Have Love And Compassion For Others

5. Properly Pay Tithes And Give Offerings

6. Believe In One God (The God Of Abraham, Isaac, And Jacob)

7. Worship Only God Almighty, The Creator Of The Universe, JESUS

8. Be Holy

9. Attend Sabbath (Friday Dark To Saturday Dark) Service(s)

10. Attend Other Service(s) When Possible

11. Make Continuous Sincere Efforts For Souls To Be Saved

12. Profess/Testify That You Must Speak In Tongues And Be Baptized In The Name Of Jesus To Be Saved

13. Profess/Testify That The Great Tribulation Is Before The Rapture

14. Reveal That Pope John Paul II Is The (Anti-Christ) Beast

15. Be Bold (Not A Coward)

16. Desire To Grow In Revelation And Power Of God

17. Be Faithful And Dedicated To The F&SF Ministry For JESUS

18. Receive/Accept The Teachings Of Apostle Frederick E. Franklin

19. Not Espouse Teachings/Doctrines Contrary To That Of Apostle Frederick E. Franklin

20. Adhere To The Leadership Of Apostle Frederick E. Franklin

21. Not Be A Liar

22. Not Be A Hypocrite

23. Not Be A Witchcraft Worker

24. Not Be A Partaker Of Idolatry

EXCERPTS FROM OUR BOOK "THE NAME OF THE (ANTI-CHRIST) BEAST AND 666 IDENTIFICATION"

There will be great deception. The scriptures indicate that the (Anti-Christ) Beast, Pope John Paul II, Carol Josef Wojtyla, will fake his death. Later on, to fake being resurrected from the dead. All to the end, to fake that he is God. All to the end, to discredit JESUS' resurrection. All to the end, to discredit that JESUS is God and rather to show/ deceive that he is God.

Revelation Ch. 17, V. 8
"...the beast that was, and is not, and yet is."

The Above scripture indicates that the Beast, Pope John Paul II, Carol Josef Wojtyla, was living. It further indicates that he will seem not to be living, but he actually will be living. He was living. He appears not to be living. But, he yet is living.

WHERE TO PURCHASE OUR BOOKS

BY APOSTLE FREDERICK E. FRANKLIN

BOOKSTORE SALES:
(25,000 BOOKSTORES)

1. BARNES & NOBLE
2. BOOKS A MILLION
3. ETC.

INTERNET SALES:
AMAZON . COM

DIRECT SALES:
2669 MEADOWVIEW DR.
MOBILE, ALABAMA 36695
PH. # : (251) 644-4329

JESUS IS GOD

1. I John Chapter 5, Verse 20

"And we know that the Son of God is come, and hath given us an understanding, that we may know him that is true, and we are in him that is true, even in his Son Jesus Christ. This is the true God, and eternal life."

2. John Chapter 1, Verses 1 & 14

"In the beginning was the Word, and the Word was with God, and the Word was God. And the Word was made flesh, and dwelt among us, (and we beheld his glory, the glory as of the only begotten of the Father,) full of grace and truth."

3. I Timothy Chapter 3, Verse 16

"And without controversy great is the mystery of godliness: God was manifest in the flesh, justified in the Spirit, seen of angels, preached unto the Gentiles, believed on in the world, received up into glory."

4. Isaiah Chapter 9, Verse 6

"For unto us a child is born, unto us a son is given: and the government shall be upon his shoulder: and his name shall be called Wonderful, Counsellor,

The mighty God, The everlasting Father, The Prince of Peace."

5. <u>Matthew Chapter 1, Verse 23</u>
"Behold, a virgin shall be with child, and shall bring forth a son, and they shall call his name Emmanuel, which being interpreted is, God with us."

6. <u>Titus Chapter 1, Verses 3 & 4</u>
"...God our Saviour;...the Lord Jesus Christ our Saviour."

7. <u>Isaiah Chapter 43, Verse 11</u>
"I, even I, am the Lord; and beside me there is no Saviour."

8. <u>Isaiah Chapter 44, Verse 6</u>
"Thus saith the Lord the King of Israel, and his redeemer the Lord of hosts; I am the first, and I am the last; and beside me there is no God."

9. <u>Revelation Chapter 1, Verses 17 & 18</u>
"...I am the first and the last: I am he that liveth, and was dead..."

10. <u>Revelation Chapter 22, Verses 13 & 16</u>
"I am Alpha and Omega, the beginning and the end, the first and the last. I Jesus have sent mine angel to testify unto you these things in the churches..."

11. <u>Isaiah Chapter 44, Verse 24</u>
"Thus saith the Lord, thy redeemer, and he that formed thee from the womb, I am the Lord that maketh all things; that stretcheth forth the heavens alone; that spreadeth abroad the earth by myself..."

12. <u>Colossians Chapter 1, Verses 16, 17 & 18</u>
"For by him were all things created, that are in heaven, and that are in earth, visible and invisible, whether they be thrones, or powers: all things were created by him, and for him: And he is before all things, and by him all things consist. And he is the head of the body the church."

13. <u>Ephesians Chapter 5, Verse 23</u>
"For the husband is the head of the wife, even as Christ is the head of the church: and he is the saviour of the body."

14. <u>Colossians Chapter 2, Verse 9</u>
"For in Him dwelleth all the fullness of the Godhead bodily."

15. <u>I John Chapter 5, Verse 7</u>
"...three that bear record in heaven, the Father, the Word, and the Holy Ghost: and these three are one."

16. <u>Revelation Chapter 15, Verse 3</u>
"...Great and Marvelous are thy works, Lord God Almighty; just and true are thy ways, thou King of saints."

17. <u>Revelation Chapter 17, Verse 14</u>
"...and the Lamb shall overcome them: for he is Lord of lords, and King of kings; and they that are with him are called, and chosen, and faithful."

18. <u>I Thessalonians Chapter 3, Verse 13</u>
"...God, even our Father, at the coming of our Lord Jesus Christ with all his saints."

19. <u>Zechariah Chapter 14, Verse 5</u>
"...and the Lord my God shall come, and all the saints with thee."

20. <u>I John Chapter 3, Verse 16</u>
"Hereby perceive we the love of God, because he laid down his life for us."

21. Etc.

<u>THE FOUR EASY STEPS TO GET SAVED/BORN AGAIN:</u>
1. Repent:

    a. ask God to forgive your sins, ask in the name of Jesus;

    b. surrender your will for God's will to be done in your life.

2. Ask God to save you, to fill you with the Holy Ghost, ask in the name of Jesus.

3. Do not ask God anymore to save you, just thank God, praise God for saving you. You must thank God in the name of Jesus. At the point of your greatest sincerity, you will speak in another language. This will be your sign of confirmation. God will be using your mouth to speak a language spoken somewhere on earth that you have not learned. This is your sign that you are born of the Spirit.

4. Get baptized in the name of Jesus Christ.

John Ch.3,Vs.3&5
"Jesus answered...Except a man be born again, he cannot see the kingdom of God...Jesus answered... Except a man be born of water and of the Spirit he cannot enter into the kingdom of God."

John Ch.3,V.8
"...thou hearest the sound thereof...so is everyone that is born of the Spirit."

Colossians Ch.3,V.17
"And whatsoever ye do in word or deed, do all in the name of the Lord Jesus..."

THE SABBATH

What Is The Sabbath?
The Sabbath is a holy day ordained by God to be so. It is a day for all to cease from work.

When Is The Sabbath?
The Sabbath is the last day, the seventh day of the week.

Genesis Ch.2, Vs. 1-3
"Thus the heavens and earth were finished, and all of the host of them. And on the seventh day God ended his work which he had made; and he rested on the seventh day from all his work which he had made."

Exodus Ch.20, Vs. 8-11
"Remember the sabbath day, to keep it holy. Six days shalt thou labour, and do all thy work: But the seventh day is the sabbath of the Lord thy God: in it thou shalt not do any work, thou, nor thy son, nor thy daughter, thy manservant, nor thy cattle, nor thy stranger that is within thy gates: For in six days the Lord made heaven and earth, the sea, and all that in them is, and rested the seventh day:

wherefore the Lord blessed the sabbath day, and hallowed it."

Exodus Ch.23, V. 12
"Six days thou shalt do thy work, and on the seventh day thou shalt rest: that thine ox and thine ass may rest, and the son of thy handmaid, and the stranger, may be refreshed."

When Does The Day Start?
The day starts at dark and goes to the next day at dark.

Genesis Ch.1, Vs 5, 8, 13, 19, 23 & 31
"...And the evening and the morning were the first day...And the evening and the morning were the second day. And the evening and the morning were the third day. And the evening and the morning were the fourth day. And the evening and the morning were the fifth day. And God saw every thing that he had made and, behold, it was very good. And the evening and the morning were the sixth day."

Is It A Sin To NOT Keep Or Violate The Sabbath?
To keep the Sabbath is one of the ten commandments. One of the ten commandments say thou shalt not kill. Another says thou shalt not steal. Just as it is sin to kill and steal, likewise, is it a sin to NOT keep or to violate the Sabbath.

Exodus Ch.20, V. 13-15
"Thou shalt not kill. Thou shalt not commit adultery. Thou shalt not steal."

What You Should Not Do On The Sabbath.
Exodus Ch.20, V. 10
"But the seventh day is the sabbath of the Lord thy God: in it thou shalt not do any work, thou, nor thy son, nor thy daughter, thy manservant, nor thy maidservant, nor thy cattle, nor thy stranger that is within thy gates..."

Nehemiah Ch.10, V. 31
"And if the people of the land bring ware or any victuals on the sabbath day to sell, that we would not buy it of them on the sabbath, or on the holy day..."

Nehemiah Ch.13, Vs. 16-18
"There dwelt men of Tyre also therein, which brought fish, and all manner of ware, and sold on the sabbath unto the children of Judah, and in Jerusalem. Then I contended with nobles of Judah, and said unto them, What evil thing is this that ye do, and profane the sabbath day? Did not your fathers thus, and did not our God bring all this wrath upon this city? Yet ye bring more wrath upon Israel by profaning the sabbath."

What Happened When The Sabbath Was Not Kept Or Violated Intentionally.

Numbers Ch.15, Vs. 32-36

"And while the children of Israel were in the wilderness, they found a man that gathered sticks upon the sabbath day. And they that found him gathering sticks brought him unto Moses and Aaron and unto all the congregation. And they put him in ward, because it was not declared what should be done unto him. And the Lord said unto Moses, The man shall be surely put to death: all the congregation shall stone him with stones without the camp. And all the congregation brought him without the camp, and stone with stones and he died; as the Lord commanded Moses."

Numbers Ch.15, Vs. 30-31

"But the soul that doeth ought presumptuously, whether he be born in the land, or a stranger, the same reproacheth the Lord; and that soul shall be cut off from among his people. Because he hath despised the word of the Lord, and hath broken his commandment, that soul shall be utterly cut off; his iniquity shall be upon."

Not Keeping Or Violating The Sabbath Out Of Ignorance.

Numbers Ch.15, Vs. 27-28

"And if any soul sin through ignorance...the priest shall make atonement for the soul that sinneth ignorantly, when he sinneth by ignorance before the Lord, to make atonement for him; and it shall be forgiven him."

Numbers Ch.15, Vs. 22, 24-25

"And if ye erred, and not observed at all these commandments...Then if it shall be, if ought be committed by ignorance without the knowledge... the priest shall make an atonement for all the congregation of the children of Israel, and it shall be forgiven them..."

Other Benefits Of Keeping The Sabbath.

God is pleased with those who obey his word and the promises of the Holy Bible is available to you.

Isaiah Ch.56 Vs. 2, 5-7

"Blessed is the man that doeth this, and the son of man that layeth hold on it; that keepeth the sabbath from polluting it, and keep his hand from doing any evil. Even unto them will I give in mine house and within my walls a place and a name better than the sons and daughters. I will give them an everlasting name, that shall not be cut off. Also the sons of the stranger that join themselves to the Lord, to serve him, and to love the name of the Lord, to be his servants, every one that keepeth the sabbath from polluting it, and taketh hold of my covenant; Even them will I bring unto my holy mountain, and make them joyful in my house of prayer...their sacrifices shall be accepted upon mine altar; for mine house shall be called an house of prayer for all people."

Exodus Ch.23, V. 12
"...thou shalt rest...be refreshed."

Exodus Ch.20, V.12
"...the Lord blessed the sabbath day, and hallowed it."

Why Has Sunday Been Chosen As The So-Called Sabbath By The So-Called Christians And Some Christians?

The Pope of 325 A.D. birth this blasphemy of changing the Sabbath day from the seventh day to the first day of the week. This blasphemous change of the sabbath to Sunday was done to have the people worship God the Almighty on the same day as the worship of the sun god. Sunday the worship of the Sun god. This blasphemous change was prophesied of in the scriptures.

Matthew Ch.24, V. 24
"For there shall arise false Christs, and false prophets, and shall shew great signs and wonders; insomuch that, if it were possible, they shall deceive the very elect."

Daniel Ch.7, V. 25
"And he shall speak great words against the most High, and shall wear out the saints of the most High, and think to change times and laws..."

Daniel Ch.8, V. 12
"An host was given him against the daily sacrifice by reason of transgression, and it cast down the truth to the ground; and it practiced and prospered."

To justify this blasphemous change, he, the Pope, had to use scriptures of the Holy Bible. He used three places in the scriptures.

Matthew Ch.28, Vs. 1-6
"In the end of the sabbath, as it began to dawn toward the first day of the week, came Mary Magdalene and the other Mary to see the sepulchre. And, behold, there was a great earthquake: for the angel of Lord descended from heaven, and came and rolled back the stone from the door, and sat upon it. His countenance was like lightning, and his raiment white as snow; And for fear of him the keepers did shake, and became as dead men. And

the angel answered and said unto the women, Fear
ye not: for I know that ye seek Jesus, which was
crucified. He is not here: for he is risen, as he said.
Come, see the place where the Lord lay."

Supposedly, because Jesus was resurrected on
the first day of the week, the sabbath should be
changed to the first day of the week.

<u>I Corinthians Ch.16, Vs. 1-3</u>
"Now concerning the collection for the saints, as I
have given order to the churches of Galatia, even so
do ye. Upon the first day of the week let every one
of you lay by him in store, as God hath prospered
him, that there be no gatherings when I come. And
when I come, whosoever ye shall approve by your
letters, them will I send to bring your liberality to
Jerusalem."

Supposedly, because Paul told them to take up
a collection on the first day of the week, this,
therefore, means that the New Testament Church's
sabbath is on the first day of the week.

<u>Acts Ch.20, V. 7</u>
"And upon the first day of the week, when the
disciples came together to break bread, Paul
preached to them, ready to depart on the morrow,
and continued his speech until midnight."

Supposedly, because the disciples came together on the first day means that they came to hear the word, and because Paul preached on the first day, supposedly, this shows that the New Testament Church had as its sabbath the first day of the week.

What ridiculous justification(s) to change the Sabbath to the first day of the week.

Scriptures Of The New Testament Refuting The So-Called Sunday Sabbath.

Let us first look at the Pope's last so-called justification, Acts Ch.20, V. 7. When the scriptures said that they came "together to break bread," it means that they came together to eat. While they were there together, Paul took this opportunity to preached to them. Like any preacher would do. Refer to the immediate following scriptures, Acts Ch.20, Vs. 8-12.

Acts Ch.20, Vs. 8-12

"And there were many lights in the upper chamber, where they were gathered together. And there sat in the window a certain young man named Eutychus, being fallen into a deep sleep: and as Paul was long preaching, he sunk down with sleep, and fell down from the third loft, and was taken up dead. And Paul went down, and fell on him, and embracing him said, Trouble not yourselves; for his life is in him. When he therefore was come up again, and had broken bread, and eaten, and talked a long while, even till break of day, so he departed. And they brought the young man alive, and were not a little comforted."

Let us now look at the Pope's I Corinthians Ch.16, Vs. 1-3, justification. Here Paul tells the Church of Corinth to give an offering to the Church in Jerusalem. He said take up collection on the first day of the week. Note that Paul said that there should not be any gathering. The people could not gather on the sabbath day to sell or give their goods or livestock to get a collection, so Paul said do it on the first day of the week. And whatever they gathered on the first day of the week, that is where their offering would come from.

Let us now look at the Pope's third and remaining justification, Matthew Ch.28, Vs. 1-6. These scriptures speak of Jesus' resurrection on the first day of they week. Somehow, this gives us the right to change God's word of a seventh day Sabbath. This is nonsense. God says that there is nothing above his word, not even the name of Jesus.

Psalm 138, V. 2
"I will worship toward thy holy temple, and praise thy name for thy lovingkindness and for thy truth:

for thou hast magnified thy word above all thy name."

Now let us see when Paul, Jews and the Gentiles, the New Testament Church, really worshipped. When their Sabbath actually was.

Acts Ch.18, V. 4
"And he reasoned in the synagogue every Sabbath, and persuaded the Jews and the Greeks"

Acts Ch.13, Vs. 13-17, 22-23, 42-44
"Now when Paul and his company loosed from Paphos...they came to Antioch...and went into the synagogue on the sabbath day, and sat down. And after the reading of the law and the prophets the rulers of the synagogue sent unto them, saying, Ye men and brethren, if ye have any word of exhortation for the people, say on. Then Paul stood up, and beckoning with his hand said, Men of Israel, and ye that fear God, give audience. The God of this people of Israel chose our fathers... he raised up unto them David to be their King... Of this man's seed hath God according to his promise raised unto Israel a Savior, Jesus...And when the Jews were gone out of the synagogue, the Gentiles besought that these words might be preached to them the next sabbath. Now when the congregation was broken up, many of the Jews and

religious proselytes followed Paul…And the next sabbath day came almost the whole city together to hear the word of God."

Note: Jews that worshipped God, only worshipped on the seventh day, the real Sabbath day.

<u>I Peter Ch.3, Vs. 15-16</u>
"But sanctify the Lord God in your hearts: and be ready always to give an answer to every man that asketh you a reason of the hope that is in you with meekness and fear: Having a good conscience; that, whereas they speak evil of you, as of evildoers, they may be ashamed that falsely accuse your good conversation in Christ."

<u>What About Colossians Chapter 2, Verse 16?</u>
<u>Colossians Ch.2, V. 16</u>
Let no man judge you in meat, or in drink, or respect of an holyday, or of the new moon, or of the sabbaths…"

There are more than one kind of sabbath referred to in the Holy Bible. There is the seventh day sabbath as has been discussed thus far and there are other sabbaths and holydays. These other sabbaths and holydays are what is referred to in Colossians Chapter 2, Verse 16. These sabbaths included the Passover, feast days, and some other holydays observed by the Jews. Among these days was The Dedication Of The Temple built by Solomon.

John Ch.10, Vs. 22-23
"And it was at Jerusalem the feast of the dedication, and it was winter. And Jesus walked in the temple in Solomon's porch."

Another such sabbath day is referred to in John Chapter 19, Verse 31.

John Ch.19, V. 31
"The Jews therefore, because it was the preparation, that the bodies should not remain upon the cross on the sabbath day, (for that sabbath was an high day,)..."

The lack of understanding of the above scripture is how the Pope of 325 A.D. has been able to deceive the people in celebrating the worship of the Spring goddess. This is the Easter celebration. Refer to our book, "Jesus Was Not Crucified When As Has Been Taught."

Here are some of the scriptures referring to the other sabbaths: Leviticus Ch.19, Vs. 1-3; Leviticus Ch.19, V. 30; Leviticus Ch.16, Vs. 29-31; Leviticus Ch.25, Vs. 1-5; Leviticus Ch.26, Vs. 27-35; Leviticus Ch.23, Vs. 4-7; Leviticus Ch.23, Vs. 15, 21, 23-28, 32-36 & 38-39; I Kings Ch.8, Vs. 63-66; etc.

These are the ordinances that Jesus blotted out, even nailing to them the cross.

SPECIAL EXCEPTIONS TO WORKING ON THE SABBATH:

People who try to get around the word of God concerning not working on the Sabbath, try to use certain instances when JESUS said it was alright to do certain things on the Sabbath. They point to the scriptures when JESUS' disciples were hungry and they plucked corn on the Sabbath. They, also, refer to the scriptures when JESUS healed on the Sabbath; the Pharisees complained that JESUS was working on the Sabbath.

EXPLANATION:

JESUS indicates his justification for the efforts on the Sabbath by two short statements.

1. In The Plucking Of Corn On The Sabbath—

JESUS says—

("The sabbath was made for man, and not man for the sabbath.")

JESUS does not want or require anyone to starve because it is the Sabbath. Refer to Mark Ch. 2, Vs. 23-28.

<u>Mark Ch. 2, Vs. 23-25&27</u>
"And it came to pass, that he went through the corn fields on the sabbath day: and his disciples began, as they went, to pluck the ears of corn. And the Pharisees said unto him, Behold, why do they on the sabbath day that which is unlawful? And he said unto them, Have ye never read what David did, when he had need, and was a hungred, he, and they that were with him? How he went into the house of God in the days of Abiathar the high priest, and did eat showbread, which is not lawful to eat but for the priest, and gave also to them which were with him? And he said unto them, The sabbath was made for man, and not man for the sabbath.

2.   In The Healing On The Sabbath—

JESUS Indicates—

(It is right to do good on the sabbath.)

During the work of God is always permitted, even on the Sabbath. Refer to Luke Ch. 13, Vs. 14,15&16.

<u>Luke Ch. 13, Vs. 14,15&16</u>
"And the ruler of the synagogue answer with indignation, because that Jesus had healed on the Sabbath day, and said unto the people, There are six days in which men ought to work: in them

therefore come and be healed, and not sabbath day. The Lord then answered him, and said, Thou hypocrite, doth not each one of you on the sabbath loose his ox or his ass from the stall, and lead him away to watering? And ought not this woman, being a daughter of Abraham, whom Satan hath bound, lo these eighteen years, be loosed from this bond on the sabbath day?"

If there is an emergency or critical need that happens the day of the Sabbath, JESUS does not expect you to ignore it. JESUS does not expect you to let someone suffer or die because it is the Sabbath. This does not include other regularly scheduled jobs or occupations on the Sabbath to meet your family needs. Ministering is always permitted, even on the Sabbath. Except for the above, the work that is not permitted on the Sabbath is work that you do on the six other days of the week.

THE FOUR EASY STEPS TO GET SAVED/BORN AGAIN:

1. Repent:

    a. ask God to forgive your sins, ask in the name of Jesus;

    b. surrender your will for God's will to be done in your life.

2. Ask God to save you, to fill you with the Holy Ghost, ask in the name of Jesus.

3. Do not ask God anymore to save you, just thank God, praise God for saving you. You must thank God in the name of Jesus. At the point of your greatest sincerity, you will speak in another language. This will be your sign of confirmation. God will be using your mouth to speak a language spoken somewhere on earth that you have not learned. This is your sign that you are born of the Spirit.

4. Get baptized in the name of Jesus Christ.

John Ch.3,Vs.3&5
"Jesus answered...Except a man be born again, he cannot see the kingdom of God...Jesus answered... Except a man be born of water and of the Spirit he cannot enter into the kingdom of God."

John Ch.3,V.8
"...thou hearest the sound thereof...so is everyone that is born of the Spirit."

Colossians Ch.3,V.17
"And whatsoever ye do in word or deed, do all in the name of the Lord Jesus..."

CONTACT PAGE

We provide this page for those of you who desire to get in contact with us regarding:

I.   Ministering
    A. Preaching
    B. Singing
    C. Being prayed for
II. Ordering tapes
    A. A. Audio of this book
    B. Preaching
    C. Singing
    D. Additional end times prophecies
III. Ordering books
IV. Questions concerning our next book
V.   Other questions.

Remember to give your address. For a quicker response, provide a telephone number where you can be reached.

Frederick & Sylvia Franklin's Ministry for JESUS
2669 Meadowview Drive
Mobile, AL, 36695
Telephone #: (251) 644-4329

ABOUT THE AUTHOR

"New York City Becomes The Capital Of The New World Order" was written by Apostle Frederick E. Franklin of the ministry of F & SF Ministry For JESUS. What has been written is revelation from God that has been given to Frederick and his wife Sylvia. Frederick E. Franklin is an apostle, prophet and end times preacher. His wife, Sylvia Franklin, is a prophetess, evangelist and singer. The ministry positions stated above are what God, himself, has said/ordained and anointed them to be. Frederick and Sylvia have three children, Elijah Jeremiah Ezekiel Franklin, Daniel Isaiah Franklin, and Rebekah Anna Franklin. Frederick E. Franklin was a successful electrical engineer in private industry, state and federal government and also self-employment, before he was born again and told by God to preach.